BRIGHT

STUP
ID

CONFE
TTI

GARY J.
SHIPLEY

Requests for permission should be directed to 1111@1111press.com, or mailed to
11:11 Press LLC, 4732 13th Ave S, Minneapolis, MN 55407.

Design by Mike Corrao

ISBN: 9781948687393 (ebook)
9781948687317 (paperback, limited edition)
9781948687614 (paperback)

Printed in the United States of America

FIRST AMERICAN EDITION

9 8 7 6 5 4 3 2 1

BRIGHT STUPID CONFETTI

GARY J. SHIPLEY

SOME OF THESE TEXTS HAVE APPEARED IN THE FOL-
LOWING PLACES: *EVERGREEN REVIEW*, *TRAGICKAL*,
AND *VESTIGES/BLACK SUN LIT.*

THE TITLE OF THIS COLLECTION, FROM PLATH'S
'YEARS', IS ALSO THE NAME OF AN EXCELLENT ONLINE
ART GALLERY CURATED BY CHRISTOPHER HIGGS.

Reading these poems, I have the constant feeling of having to catch up to their speaker. He strides ahead of me and beckons with his head. Comparisons are made, often to astronomy, climatology, genetics, computing, medicine, animal studies, but Shipley has already leapt over the fences of the metaphors. These prose poems have the elegance of both scientific proofs and the Goldberg Variations. They offer no answers but the wry humor of their own making and unmaking. As Laozi taught, and Shipley demonstrates again and again, the way that can be communicated is not the way, but still we wish to communicate.

— Jee Leong Koh, author of *Connor & Seal*

In its form, tropes, tone, and intensity, Bright Stupid Confetti joins a nightray of decadent prose running from Baudelaire to José Antonio Ramos Sucre to Johannes Göransson. This volume explores the hope/fear that the body can discover more of itself, and that the voice uttered in the chasm of one's own bodily dream-terrain may pronounce an infernal logic to blot out the sun. "The sound of yourself: that storm of barbed wire." A book to curl up with.

— Joyelle McSweeney, author of *The Red Bird* and *Flet*

For all its formal beauty and gut-wrenching images, what I find most fascinating about Gary J Shipley's writing is its perpetual endeavor to penetrate the impenetrable, which is to me the very definition of tautology—*and* of obsession. There is a kind of concentrated narrativity in these pure ruminations that I relish. If there really is something beyond the language, it has to be either pointless, or bizarre. And that's all part of the game. Nonsenseness is not senselessness. Read any of Shipley's work, and you'll get it.

— Róbert Gál, author of *Agnomia* and *Naked Thoughts*

Gazing at Shipley's book, you might ask: what kind of genetic variant material is this? Is it torture-torn? Is it Martian friendly? Is it beauty dressed like microgravity or permafrost or burqa? Perhaps everything Shipley writes is a type of Ethiopian digitalized wolf: remote-controlled, ferocious, savagely fierce. His blocks of prose move like wolves hunting in packs, pursuing cloning and animal instincts for demonstrative gut bacteria or survival, seeking to 3D print pointlessness on one sheet of text that could be called your soul. Shipley prunes our eyesight where a million epileptic trees of perceptions sprout. Perhaps he has written a book for the sleep-tortured, for three cats, for fog, for global warming, for a whale in an embryo, for your genetic abnormality, for your favorite nosebleed, for your rice paddies, for your death fixation, for your immunosuppressants, for your cephalopodic crocodile, or just simply for you because you love the genetic material of language so much or perhaps to give you what you deserve the most: "temporal indigestion."

— Vi Khi Nao, author of *Fish in Exile* and *Sheep Machine*

For ESO

TABLE OF CONTENTS

YET AGAIN	13
THE CHAMBER	14
AEGIS	15
BODY OF A NOBODY	16
SENSATE AS A MEANS	17
PROXIMITY	18
NO SEASONS	19
TUNNELING	20
LEGIBLE?	21
VISIONS	22
FOOTNOTES	23
THE NEW HUMANS	24
ATTENTION TO THE PRESENT	25
TRACES OF ERASURE	26
EMOTICON	27
THE BODY OF ELISA LAM	28
THE DESTINATION MYTH	29
THE LAST GOD	30
SATELLITES	31
THE HUM WE SANG	32
GOLD, AS IT WERE	33
JUNGLESE	34
THE WORLD OUTSIDE	35
VOLCANOLOGY	36
APRICOTS	37
GESTURES	38

CLIMATES 39

BACKGROUND 40

THE ELEPHANT'S LUNG 41

XY 42

THE DECOMMISSIONED WALKER 43

THE INTERROGATION 44

FOG 45

THAW 46

DISQUIETUDE 47

THE IDEA OF A FLY 48

SELF-DIAGNOSIS 49

ONLY IN PARADISE 50

EPIPHENOMENA 51

BY WAY OF CONCLUSION 52

SMOTHER 53

NATURE 54

ACEDIA REVISITED 55

AUTOPSY OF A DOLPHIN 56

THE REPRIEVE 57

MARTIAN WINTER 58

OFF CAMERA 59

VIGIL 60

BRIGHT STUPID CONFETTI 61

AQUARIUM 63

THE ART OF ART 64

PROBLEMS OF CONSCIOUSNESS 65

WOLF-MAN 66

BOUBA AND KIKI 67

THE COLOUR OF SPACE 68

KANGAROOS 69

THE PRETENCE OF WATER 70

FRIDGE NOISE 71

FORM AND CONTENT 72

BIPEDAL 73

A VISIT TO CHEN 74

PLEASE LOOK 75

FINGERMARKS 76

SIMILE 77

NOCTURNE 78

ROUTES 79

SOLIDS 80

BEYONDS WITH THIS HOUR 81

RHYMING PANG 82

AN EXILE 83

EMPORIUM 84

MEMORANDUM 85

HALF-LIFE 86

MY FAVORITE NOSEBLEED 87

PROSTHETICS 88

STAIRWELLS 89

THIS COMPARATIVE SAMENESS 90

DIAGNOSTICS 91

EMPTY INTERIORS 92

COLLAPSE NOISE 93

LOGISTICS 94

A VISIT TO HERE 95

CONCERNING THIS 96

CONTINGENT ON 97

THE OTHERNESS OF OTHERNESS 98

NOT THE ONE YOU GIVE 99

TEMPORAL INDIGESTION 100

COMMUNITY 101

VIRAL 102

OUTSIDE AESTHETICS 103

WHAT WE GET TO SEE 104

INAPPROPRIATE COSTUME 105

THE END OF LUNCH, ALMOST 106

THE EXPERIMENT 107

DAISY 108

SKINNED ALIVE 109

CODA 110

Yes, in the long run there is something to be said for these shiftless days, each distilling its drop of poison until the cup is full; there is something to be said for them because there is no escaping them.

John Ashbery

YET AGAIN

Was that you simultaneously falling apart in the middle and at the edges? And after all that, it turned out relatively harmless. Your lifespan spanned a life just the same. And what had been shown to work in mice worked in you. Those tornadoes on the sun never made the difference you dreamed they'd make. The air pollution got everyone, and you as well, if you'd bothered to breathe. Then there's the head you wore as a head, and how no one thought to mention that. Did you paint it invisible in the hope of being seen? The way I see it, no one has futility on their death certificate, and it's not for want of trying.

THE CHAMBER

No one bird evades me. The sun brought no extra sadness, no extra sound. How could it? There is no soundless key to open sound. There are only those rooms of those scientists—where everyone goes mad. It takes a certain time of not hearing anything: that's it, nothing else. The sound of yourself: that storm of barbed wire. And no day and no night. And the unheard shriek of something never intended to be listened to. This is no deprivation of the deaf, but the concentrative excess of something else. And nothing survives that.

AEGIS

Our software programs talk among themselves, and we do not care that we do not understand. For we are no longer in line for bread. We have eaten and are eaten and the secrets beyond us aren't even secrets anymore. Any harm we're owed is calculated in advance and forgotten in the service of any one instant—which can last until the next, whether it arrives or not.

BODY OF A NOBODY

There is an emerging body of research. It leaks dark, foul-smelling secretions. It is dragging a leg. Nobody is doing anything on purpose. Nobody is fasting for the other world. I'm imagining a fetal shark swimming in circles in its mother's uterus till it dies. How it dies without maturing. How sometimes the holiest places are the ones we're trapped in. It's funny the way, while sneezing, I eschew a tissue. It's funny the way you confront yourself at your own risk. I plan to go bald, and from that baldness make a noose of human hair. I plan the mass expansion of deserts. I hear tiny white crabs purring in the sand. The difference might not sound like much, but I'm awake before I hit the pillow.

SENSATE AS A MEANS

I remember that whatever's numb is there to be chewed off—without the numb thing knowing. I explain my collapse by refusing to collapse. And the antidote to this panic isn't me. My eyes are wider too than all the people that are breathless. What cannot be said gets said anyway. And because of this my proficiency with silence feels unnatural. I have eyes all over my body: they are there even in my blood, and being alive doesn't require some or all of them to close.

PROXIMITY

All Xs will do Y when exposed to Z. I have no money, but how much for the (life you promised me)? I'm not saying anything new, but can you do me the courtesy of listening anyway? You see, it's the temple I'm in that's sensing where the bolt gun goes. It's there like this phantom limb, growing from my head. So far, so shuffling backwards towards the edge. My perturbations are just so very slightly different from your own. Can't we go someplace together and never arrive? We can blame the drag effect of our bodies. We can act as though our lice are better than theirs. Can't we pretend to be asleep, and leave our brains across our pillows—execution-style? It seems to me I'm making like I'm making all this up. And why not, when it's precisely the thing in front of me that I'm after.

NO SEASONS

The lives you're all living: I don't believe them. I imagine the world as if I'm dying in private. There's so little left it fills a million churches. A million stadium-sized churches filled with countless emptinesses outgrowing the air. There's a notion of going that I like, and I am more often ludic there, for it seems like a place. And while I have no seasons, and do not describe the world, I have airlessness and the air's overabundant return. I have the idea I'm breathing.

TUNNELING

By now I'm quite the mass delusion. I don't know whether I'm pretending to be myself or pretending to be myself pretending. Ach, what's the *différance*? When I was young I went dynamite fishing for compliments. And then my flexible camouflage wasn't flexible anymore. And then it wasn't camouflage anymore. Unlike rabbits, human females do not absorb their unborn children. As a consequence, I'm not sure in which direction to dig the tunnel: which way is back? which way forward? which way out? I have a disguise in a bag tied to my ankle. A non sequitur won't cut it, so I use my teeth instead.

LEGIBLE?

When buildings explode with people inside them, I plan to feel something—something more than my own expediency to myself. The language comes apart in similar ways. Limbs fly off at angles I can't predict. There are bits of faces and skin, and teeth gone from mouths, organs left functionless on floors and none of it comes together—or needs to. The air around and between is so vast it echoes. If I capture it alive, which is more difficult than it sounds, its uvulars draw blood. Clearing my throat, the spatter pattern looks like something I could read without knowing.

VISIONS

The blind shall have light inside their eyes, and will not miss the other source. Blindness is horrifying, because nobody has anywhere else to live. I have many sentences built from this miracle, and I get to feel them when I like. Alternatively, an anesthetic for living isn't supposed to replace the living, but the difference remains unclear. His pulse, he said, was one of a list of similarly subtle impairments. As a visual artist with only partial sight, he aestheticized his depictive anomalies. When the last thing left to decide is whether to blindfold or not, demand both.

FOOTNOTES

In my other language, the fog is always yellow and the light is the light of afternoons. The trains are always silent, and derailed, and the men on bicycles, circling the crash site, are never only that: they are growing into one another, like men into cockroaches and cockroaches into women. A Frenchman watches a parade while hanging from his belt, and the fog comes in, the colour of mustard, the colour of children // with kidney disease laughing in the other language at the men's faces turning blue, turning purple, turning black, turning soft. And I'm pissed rotten pissing blood in the Hofgarten until I collapse, and I never have to wake up, and when it rains nothing is compelled to grow. Or else it grows the other way, so we don't have to see it: a garden under the ground, stretching for miles, stretching for the sake of stretching, like the dogs on the mud, their tails in the air, forbidden to dig, and growling, and drained of air.

THE NEW HUMANS

In our laboratories we will make new humans. They
will be better adapted to the otherness. They will
have the darkest eyes—a decompositional darkness—
so large and so dark they are hard to look at and see
anything but their unchecked seeing. We will come to
feel quarantined in their company. And such benign
condescension in the looks they'll give us, such well-
intentioned pity for not being them. When there's
talk of how they are using their own language, we'll
have no choice. We will learn to miss them without
wanting to.

ATTENTION TO THE PRESENT

At three seconds to midnight the mangrove forest
will glow in the dark. All but one of a troop of male
chimpanzees will tear off their sexual organs and
stoically contemplate a river. The lovers left in the
houses left will stand face to face like concrete curios
and breathe. A grey squirrel will eat the unprocessed
brain of another grey squirrel. A boy in West Africa,
with sleeping sickness, will wake up just in time.
Thousands of nightingales will circle a temple. A
handful of spiders will congregate in a hand. A mother
will lie to a child and smile. The smile will not look
like any smile he's ever seen. At the back of a drawer
a forgotten Tamagotchi will beg for food.

TRACES OF ERASURE

My biography from before remains unaltered. Only, there's a different me for every failing, every ignorance, every sad error—the biography of a colony. And still the boy-version mistakes the taste of batteries for blood, and still another version sees itself as the central importunity of its current age. And of the maladjustments in my head, and from there all over (me, everyone, all things), of the material mental illness I'd become, as something deranged on the all-too-clear view and of the eventual detumescence, the endless plateau of the thing all of a sudden healed wrongly of itself, there's this, this nothing of an explanation... and gone now the last version, and with it the sense that any of us needed recording.

EMOTICON

The emotions are played out. Seriously, who cares if your heart disintegrates like week-old cake, or century-old teeth, whether it's held together with synthetic glue or re-used parcel tape? Or whether instead of your heart it's your brain or your spleen or the inexactitude of your longings? The emoticon is enough. Even the emoji's too much. Thing is: the more we talk about them, the less there's anything there to talk about. If I don't come home tomorrow, it's the law of diminishing returns. Thing is: I'm alone so much I forget that any of this has any relevance. Take a moment and save them for some imagined future, and for all the rest of it there's a surgeon's description of a tumour.

THE BODY OF ELISA LAM

On her way to turning up naked in a tank, she had a map to follow in San Diego Zoo. Still, there's every reason to believe she was lost inside. And an unknown number of people were watching a certain Japanese horror film the day she arrived in Los Angeles. And somebody else was complaining about the oddness of water. Incalculably many others were wasting their lives without ever being haunted. In the elevator video she presses all the floors at once, and when the doors won't close she leaves. Her psychomotor agitation presupposes no interlocutor. In the Lost Forest there were hippos swimming. When I imagine them, they look scared and directionless. A hippo's yawn is meant as a threat. Only something without a voice would ever need a mouth that big.

THE DESTINATION MYTH

I would say things like, *I oscillate between systems I don't believe in and a randomness in which I don't exist*, and *I only dream of the dreams I don't have. The ones I want because I don't have them*. And it sounded dramatic put like that, but it took so long to formulate that all the urgency was gone. And so I made this point of making pointlessness the point, and when that seemed pointless, it consolidated my point, and just how pointless it was. I did all this in the hope that I'd forget what I had done. In the hope that I could remain hopeless for a while. Imagine: all that effort and no manger at the end of it.

THE LAST GOD

My god is an atheist—the agnostic kind, which is all of us. He's the only god I can stomach. There was a time when he believed, before his crisis of faith. But now he's all self-doubt and see-through, and oddly easier to behold. He is the sky over Greenland watching his incurables find the wrong cure. He is a megalodon swallowed by a goldfish. It would take a supercomputer a million years to not understand him correctly. What remains of his host organism is incubated in his mouth; it's why he mumbles, and why he's thought to think his thoughts out loud.

SATELLITES

What if all you have is the idea? And readiness-to-hand feels like a distance? And the thing is no longer tangible? When we're alone I feel only the idea of your body. All sensuousness becomes erasure: the collision of our two nothings. I wonder, what if my fictions aren't about anything at all. What if they just are? I realize then that no act of intimacy is so close that my thinking can't insinuate the union. Reality is a bird flying upside down to the moon, and finding its nest instead. You talk the moon; I don't see it. The moon doesn't breathe. I see your thinking of the moon like it might become your mind, as if a mind existed that was not the moon already.

THE HUM WE SANG

The present stammers for years before commencing at some removed time and place much the same as where it started. And whatever I am is waiting at the end of some almost infinite lag. Who here can separate events: a day, a year, the start of a disease, the end of it, the extremities of love? If I sit here long enough my fingernails will fall apart, and nobody will be able to tell when it was the human gave way to its consciousness of itself.

GOLD, AS IT WERE

We'll reminisce fondly on all the animals we killed. We'll build petting zoos from all the simulated meats. And afterwards, after everything, we'll remember our kisses ingested like a fist. But then somebody's bound to lament how much better it was, back when the things we put inside us were real. How you could taste the verity back then. People used to go outside, remember? We'd walk places and the weather wasn't ours. The cancers bloomed in our lungs and our heads, and we turned our mattresses in spring.

JUNGLESE

Mutilated figures of the latest war spool into an old cartoon. There are creatures exploding with health. I hear the bomb-making factories through the canopy. I hear the fungus on the floor. I have the orangutan-eyed view: the maimed walking below like newborn giraffes, their routes back home so many intricately mangled circles. I'm such an odd-shaped arboreal bird: too heavy to fly, no wings, too full of air to fall without bouncing. Every night I build a nest for the last time. From the jungle understory I wait for the blast. When it comes I'll ask them if my genitals are still there, and nobody will answer.

THE WORLD OUTSIDE

My punishment for thinking is the grogginess of my surroundings. I could gain 100 pounds of who I am. My thoughts read the way a helicopter talks. I'm some profanity of now, some ancientness of never. I walk every day just to sleep at night. I sleep every night just to walk the next day. The sunshine is darkest when I open my eyes. I see where I'm going like any other excuse for movement. I'm so boundless and microscopic I'm beyond my own imagining. My vertebrae are crunching like glow sticks. I put things out of my mind only to find them again: in rooms, in furniture, in walls. That I find no meaning becomes the meaning. That I never find what isn't there is my propensity for looking.

VOLCANOLOGY

Maybe it's too early to tell, but this feels like the control. And it's all these others got the treatment. I mean, what's the point of 86 billion neurons (give or take) when you're hiding in the throat of a volcano? (Hölderlin knew to keep Empedocles out, but who am I to listen to my betters.) And do they ever study the effect in rats of what it takes to just wake up every day? Still no one shouts me from the juniper forests. We are all of us old and our friends are dying. I was misdiagnosed at birth with that selfsame event. Imagine: only this long, dreamless sleep and the high survival rate of nobody we knew.

APRICOTS

If there were ever apricots in my skin, they are not there now. Or perhaps they turned bad along the way, and are now so soft, so macerated, that I cannot distinguish them from the surrounding flesh. But then I'm not so sure they were ever there. I never could swallow the world without chewing. And no doubt it's symptomatic of a failing, but while you're at it, could you check the bite marks in my colon. And perhaps nothing about me was ever ripe in time. Perhaps there was no skeleton in the jellyfish. Perhaps the apricots were someone else's all along.

GESTURES

The pelagic bird looks out and doesn't bother. The sea is too far and just more land at the end of it. The cat has melted into the pavement; the cow, somewhere back there, has given up on grass. The bee stops, falls out the air; the tortoise has forgotten he's alive. I breathe smoke into the lungs of the last ape, and all the flies inside her suffocate.

CLIMATES

A polar bear dies of hypothermia in the middle of summer. All the flowers are sucked back into the soil in spring. When autumn ends the trees are no less green. And for what it's worth, winter happened yesterday and now it's gone. Aren't there places where it's always summer, always winter? I mean, it's all just weather, right? And things waking up and other things not? Yet, all the impeccable nuances I read are still there, where someone left them. If I go outside, will I even notice myself?

BACKGROUND

I feel an obligation to mention my previous death
by drowning. It's only fair. Else you'll be distracted,
wondering why I look the way I do: why my eyeballs
are pruned, and there's this fine white froth around
my mouth and nose, why I gurgle when I breathe and
am prone when agitated to floating regardless of this
heavy coat, its pockets filled with rocks and sand. And
my smile, you're right, is not unlike the *Inconnue*—
like the accession to the accident, and then the plot,
had settled there and spread.

THE ELEPHANT'S LUNG

He forgets how many strains of madness he overcame—every day, over and over, with order, with routine, with crannies of thought filled with softened light—and how it turned his face a yellowed, greenish white, as if all that time spent looking away arrived at once to make this undiagnosable state. And he vomited and couldn't breathe, and somewhere hidden in this process another voice arrived, excerpted from the lack of air.

XY

I saw some real humans once. Their algorithms were a joke. They claimed to have subtle differences that I couldn't see and that they couldn't explain. Some admitted to shooting ducks and elephants with Kalashnikovs, others to the cloning of Ethiopian wolves. When I showed them my 3D printed organ, they laughed like we'd been friends for centuries. They said, There's a reason male genitalia so often look like instruments of torture, but you, our friend, have missed the point entirely.

THE DECOMMISSIONED WALKER

The man in the municipal park says he's been infected for years. He tells anyone that passes, in case they're curious, about his sack-cloth suit and the teeth in the pockets he's extracted from his mouth. His piety is so convincing that when he mentions the girl he killed, some years ago, in Tuscany, I believe him straightaway. I believe too that the bite mark on his arm would match the contours of her jaw. And I believe he does not hope to turn again. I believe he does not hope to turn. I believe because the three white cats around his feet have steadily eaten them away, and because the bones inside I see are black, and because he'll need to look ahead forever just to keep from standing up.

THE INTERROGATION

The sleep-deprived are disproportionately disposed to false confession. I read it. There are studies. There is evidence. There are thousands of years in jail because of it. And I know the guilt of my own insomnia. And I know most of all that it's mine, how it makes itself mine. I know when I stare through my eyelids all night, and the next and the next, I'll take the blame for anything. I'll confess genocide, environmental ruin, the torture of innocents, every viral epidemic. I'll confess Zanzibar's 10,000 flies and the roads made from bodies in Siberia. And so what if nobody believes me, or is even listening, so long as I'm punished someplace else.

FOG

The way it happened, there was nothing in the fog. There was just the fog and the things I made from fog. But then, the way it happened, everything I made I made from that nothing—that nothing that the fog obscured, and in its own way showed. Before the fog: fog. After the fog: more fog. I didn't go into the fog looking for fog; that was my mistake.

THAW

It's been argued that warm climates impair cognitive performance. I too cannot think straight in the sun. The heat reminds me that my head is still attached, to something more forgiving of itself; and that for all my levitations in the cold, the place to die is in the warm—where all the preparatory work's been done, where all the fears have been remembered and ignored, and what is left is healthy again without ever having been sick.

DISQUIETUDE

I predict none of your typical genetic abnormalities
as my own. My radiation sickness is sui generis to a
fault. Think of this as a kind of automaton's lament.
What else is going on here if not a disease so rare
nobody ever contracted it, and finding yourself dying
of it anyway? A dog they trained to sniff out our
epilepsy, our wrongly copied cells, is licking at my
hand. What it's found it cannot say. It's code, I think,
for when there's nothing wrong exactly, but it takes a
different kind of nose to make it true.

THE IDEA OF A FLY

A young Russian boy once kissed a fly on its cheek. He grew up and learnt that flies do not have cheeks, and that what he'd kissed was just an idea. And while that was enough, it was also the taste of his future wife. Only after a routine medical procedure uncovered significant traces of hemolymph beneath his skin did anyone suspect that his habit of sleeping on the ceiling was anything other than a gravitational eccentricity. That he would routinely vomit on his food was likewise something that underwent increased scrutiny around this time. When Gogol burnt the second part of *Dead Souls* in 1852, he burnt with it a handful of incomplete short stories. This, in outline, is one of them. No one knows how it ends, in lieu of its ending.

SELF-DIAGNOSIS

There's this saying, among sufferers of Cotard's syndrome, about how realizing you're dead is the best evidence of your immortality. Of course, to be aware of your deadness is to turn yourself into a paradox. Why else do it, if not as a solution? And what better way of answering that other seminal cliché, than by turning a disjunction into a conjunction? And the problem is, I get it: I've existed where I wasn't, talked without talking, eaten without eating, been kissed at as if I was air. It's the version of *The Sixth Sense* in which Bruce Willis never works it out, in which there is no troubled boy, no wedding video, no ring. The version in which there's only him, living like he does, and no one there to tell the difference.

ONLY IN PARADISE

When Cioran was a child he played football with human skulls. This was something you could do in paradise back then, in the early part of the 20th century. For only in paradise are our heads both real enough to kick and empty enough for us not to care.

EPIPHENOMENA

Someone in a forest in Japan wants to leave without going through with it. One of 1 million a year doesn't capture the perceived uniqueness of his distaste. He knows that if he could bring himself to cry, every one of his tears would be the first of its kind since the birth of the universe.

BY WAY OF CONCLUSION

At least 100 people were killed and 400 more injured when everything continued as normal. We sat and prayed for an early diagnosis of our partial melting. The hope is that we'll soon be under water, where our dementias can't get us. Maybe the climate solution is not the mutual embarrassment of an entire species. Maybe it's not even a solution. I hunt for a new particle in the flavor notes of carbon dioxide. I conclude without doubt that this conclusion is the best conclusion I've had all day.

SMOTHER

For all the violent expirations in unroadworthy
minivans, there are people keeping themselves as
pets. It's 1957 and Curt Richter is drowning rats.
If you've been saved once, chances are you'll need
saving again. And just because it's getting harder
to breathe doesn't mean the hands around your
neck aren't exotic states of matter. Doesn't mean a
botched lethal injection is anything but a cosmetic
intervention. I wonder, did you screen my embryo so
no one could see it? Was I vanishingly small? Was I
scarified to resemble a crocodile? Was I this selfsame
meaningless loop?

NATURE

A shadow moves in the wind instead of the object. I sip at the effect of my drink. My sexual orientation is latex. You have to ask yourself who it is you're talking to. All my organs were transplanted from the same donor: a small boy who deserved better than this. And even if he didn't, a man my age is no kind of home.

ACEDIA REVISITED

I have tried to get excited by my boredom, but I only get as far as imagining what more-bored versions of myself might do. How they might be made to act. I've imagined that the most acute sensation of it wouldn't debilitate quite so much. I've imagined an agile corpse. I've sung a celebratory dirge. I've lied for the end of truth. But I became more bored and imagined I'd imagined it. And I failed to get excited about how excited I'd become. As if excitement was just my body doing things by itself. So far it's taken years off me. I'm embryonic and praying someone else gets born instead.

AUTOPSY OF A DOLPHIN

There's a thin line between the autopsy of a dolphin and my surfacing to breathe. Microgravity or not, I'm refusing to float. That's a lot of scars just to arrive at a redefinition. That's a long migration just to arrive at someone else's redemption. And yet, oddly you might think, I'm not the type to colonize a planet: my skill set is an individualism that's yet to be tested on animals. My metallicity's a paradox: what's light is also heavy, what's heavy is also light. I'm looking beyond the Standard Model, and finding more order not less. An inversion of the way I've lived, I want the destination without the getting there.

THE REPRIEVE

I am genuinely optimistic that my death from
bleeding will occur as an inevitable consequence of
some enlightened neglect. A letting calmly stretched
and then forgotten. And the pressure inside my head
will not be the pressure inside a star. Meanwhile,
the man sitting in this chair believes his thoughts
sufficiently plastic to never biodegrade. And he sits
here until that's the one thing he cannot believe.
It's funny, but through all of this he still has lifelike
eyes, a lifelike mouth, a lifelike life. An alien fauna is
growing over his groin without making a sound. He
doesn't notice. The light is outside and riddled with
small depressions. He tries to make something from
the parts he has, and like elasticity it will not mean
what we think it means.

MARTIAN WINTER

My extremities are in danger. I can sense it coming: this Martian winter. And so I've plans in place for when it happens. When the ends of my fingers turn black and smell and hurt until I cannot feel them, and then snap off. When, phalanx by phalanx, they're subtracted from and my hands are open all the time. Same thing with the toes and then I cannot walk. And then the plan is there, right where I left it, in the geometric centre of my head.

OFF CAMERA

I'm switching off all the hidden cameras. When the permafrost thaws, what's underneath will come back to life. Not the animals but what killed them. This is not my ancestral land; my ancestral land is a sliding morgue tray inside an armoire. I've quarantined the hope of the world inside this black hole. You can think of me as the event horizon. I watch the wolves and hyenas try to scale the escarpment. I watch them fail. I see through the cameras I switched off. I see how it is they are seen. I see all the heads that have forgotten their faces. I see them hiding for a place to search.

VIGIL

My loved ones are shouting down hallways in a panic
in another house. Watching them like this is like
robbing graves, where the humans have turned to
quadrupeds in their boxes, and the nervous energy
of light threatens the time-locked incubation of an
eye. I am evolving in isolation: I have night vision
and cooling blood, I have perpetuity and sadness.
The spider in the glass downstairs is circling. We are
rubbing off on one another for as long as it takes. The
invasive species is any individual not seeking a cure,
for which my waking up in the dark is an obvious
ruse.

BRIGHT STUPID CONFETTI

O God, I am not like you
In your vacuous black,
Stars stuck all over, bright stupid confetti.
Eternity bores me,
I never wanted it.

Sylvia Plath, *Years*

So much for absolute zero. So much for this monstrous, beautiful mess. We think of death as something that only happens once. We are seeing in the dark. We are recognizing emotion in faces. The impertinence of a body: it's all in your head.

A spider wants to fuck a moth. The cow is getting stranger. A type of African frog regrows its severed legs with no feet. My growing feet without the legs is like when I mistake a night sky for my reflection, and we pretend like we're the same thing—both eaten from the inside out.

Fish crawled up on to dry land about 400 million years ago. So far so unremarkable. So far and yet so vaguely human. And so this gallows humour of deep space has too many punchlines and just the one joke. When it comes to something this vast, this bleak, we're running out of new ways round it.

My less than pristine interior is a meaningless

squiggle. The plan is to release me back into the wild. But all the anti-rejection drugs are too many, too sugary. For reasons we don't understand, the transplanted organ will find its way home.

Turns out my intestinal worms are wasted here: such a useless beauty, such aerobatic loops. So many collapsing stars and no one willing to see them. They say the interview room is plain because it reduces embellishments: turns out the inside of your forgetfulness is the oldest light in the universe.

It's getting harder to find signs of life. The sun is going to explode and we'll have us an X-ray of God. But the shadow's not what you think. It's not what's always or what's fleeting, but this wedding that's boring me to death. I never wanted such an awkward silence, but now that it's here...

AQUARIUM

The sea is drowning all the fish. What else were you expecting? That the colonoscopy would find a nesting bird, perhaps. Or that those thoughts about your thoughts referred to somewhere else. What if what's missing is nothing's missing? What if the water remembers who we are, and stops? The sea is drowning all the fish. What comes next is for its own sake.

THE ART OF ART

The future of art is the same as before: it's supersymmetry, it's both beautiful and nowhere. When everyone's saying how they can't relate, I wonder, are our fecal transplants getting lost in translation. But the future takes more patience than that. And no one said echolocation would be easy. What's new if not this nestling, fed on heartburn? I say, Look! Quick! A cliché is being born. It takes seconds, and then there's another one. The first known drawing made by human hands is 73,000 years old, and it looks like anything you want.

PROBLEMS OF CONSCIOUSNESS

We need to build a chemical brain in order to
understand why we don't need one. You show me
your consciousness and I'll show you mine. If they get
on, maybe we could leave them to it. You give me a
look that says, If I ever wake up will I be there to see
it? Perhaps, perhaps I reply: there are even liquids
now that can hold a shape. If it happens this way, I'm
thinking back over all those non-conscious emotions,
and how everything I see is the wind in the trees.

WOLF-MAN

Sooner or later I will remain where I am. Lycanthropic today, eating my own faeces tomorrow. What is different seems the same, and what is the same seems precariously so. The world this way corrected in its wrongness. All your evil is too slippery, all your goods so sorry for themselves. To start with, I'm disguised like any other humanitarian. But no one sets out to drink themselves lucid. All they want to do is look at the sky—and own it. In the end, it wasn't what you'd call a page-turner, but the pages turned anyway.

BOUBA AND KIKI

After the diagnosis I forget. I need a second opinion, a third, a fourth, one for every day. Funny how they're all the same. It's a shame, but I'm not quick enough to be a hoax. My con is so long I'll pass it down to my children. And for obvious reasons there are no benign art projects. Although, conditioned taste aversion does make the eyeballs easier to digest. Lucky for me I have a protean diet. In other words, I repeat the same words. But which of these two shapes is the product of your incest? Is it Bouba or is it Kiki? Look closely! See, there, she has her mother's missing teeth.

THE COLOUR OF SPACE

The objects are moving away. They will exist in other places where they will reflect light in dissimilar ways. Someone will say they have changed colour. This alone is enough to vindicate injecting dye into the brains of mice. The effect is bluer than before. The team observed the impact on astronomers of assimilating so much space, and not one of them thought the cerebellum of a mouse could move them in the direction they were going.

KANGAROOS

All the signs are that the all-too-human must be supplemented by the latest technology. We find ourselves in bed with headaches much larger than our heads. We are driving cars wondering who is to blame. It's our bone-loss makes us so similar-looking. In civilized circles that's called a feedback loop. If we feel what it's like to feel what it's like, we call that uncanny. They mixed mind-control with our degraded motor functions and called it something else. That we continued to see in the dark was immediately hailed as a miracle. By turns it turns out and we feel most like ourselves. And we care for our young like we'd meant it all along, like it didn't mean anything to keep them warm this way: inside us like they never happened.

THE PRETENCE OF WATER

You were one side of a digital waterfall and I was the other. You said everything you thought was normal in nature felt abnormal in you, that you were biologically squeamish on an industrial scale. I said, I have doctored my blood samples to seem less crocodilian, and the result is this smile. We didn't know which of us was accumulating cell damage at the faster rate, or if the waterfall could be made to care. When the time came, we passed through each other on our way to becoming the same thing.

FRIDGE NOISE

The volunteers were shown the shapes of dreams they'd had that they couldn't remember having. From the outside, they seemed like any other breed of insect, standing upright, chewing the faces off men. Each one emphatic till the end: I was not built for this. But the drought presaged a flood, and the flood a drought. And nobody happened on their own. Think of it this way, someone said: to people with incurable diseases, even the noise of a fridge has its own incremental cost.

FORM AND CONTENT

They went into a room and ran simulations of my immortality. An hour later they came out shaking their heads. I had what they called a deeply personal response. From the inside it felt less so, like someone termite fishing for anything at all.

BIPEDAL

Compared to other bipeds I'm positively arachnid.
Always more legs than places to go, always this double
life on all fours. The poetry of reality reads like the
proceedings of a brain fluke. The poetry of reality is
not the reality of poetry. Me: I have the inertia of gold.
It's what happens to hydraulics if you let the pressure
out. But still, I'm unseasonably young. I imagine a fly
that looks like a photograph. The universe, at least,
knows when to stop. I learn to avoid open spaces
and amber. I learn to avoid being seen. I come here
dressed like a man who, from bitter experience, has
avoided the cliché of a flesh-eating horse.

A VISIT TO CHEN

Traditional Chinese medicine wants to put me back together. I am not so many discrete parts going wrong in isolation as I thought. My anatomy not some suppressed impurity of mind. I stick out my tongue and there I am clinging to its surface. My sadness is discovered in my stomach and then my toes. Turned out the bioluminescence in my head was just my kidneys acting up, and there was something I could take. The only trouble is is what the trouble is, and my struggling to struggle to understand.

PLEASE LOOK

Look at your disproportionately infinite yawn. I see now: there's nothing coming the other way. Look at your blood, all stretched out—like slow cinema. I see your eyes themselves have eyes. I see our ghosts have ghosts. Look at your brain there in the pickle jar. See, it still has the label on. Look, please look, at your heart rate on the wall—squashed flat. I see you: you're coming back to life in the seam on my sleeve. Look, look at your love at first sight gone suddenly blind. See, it's raining outside. Look at your feet. Look at your feet. See, they're shaped like the sky.

FINGERMARKS

The underweight baby becomes the overweight corpse, and what happens in between is why I sleep with my eyes open. If I had to define what it is I'm doing, I'd decline on the grounds of diminished sensitivity— not mine, yours. What's that you say? If smugness were a virtue I'd be eating my scabs by now. That's as perhaps, but how's it possible to take too much pride in one's immoderate deficiency in the stuff? And yet, it seems, you've found my soft spot, and got your fingers stuck. But someone's got to tell you, so here it is: that's no way to treat a newborn's skull. And what about my son? He's here with me. He's saying, The rhesus monkey in the research lab is screaming itself a new brain. And now look what you've made me do. My hands are all over this poem: poor thing.

SIMILE

You ask me what it feels like, like a list of similes would do it. Like one by one they'll aggregate the likenesses into some haecceity you can own. Like I'll try, if you like, like so: Like the cadaver at its autopsy—waking up. Like the end of *Tokyo Story*. Like the thought of my dead son, who isn't dead. Like brain cancer in my rectum. Like rectal cancer in my brain cancer. Like the TV in a rest home. Like a snail in a uterus. Like a woman born as a man inside a man born as a woman. Like the end of *Tokyo Story* reshot by Harmony Korine. Like Harmony Korine directed by Ozu. Like bacteria perched on a cliff. Like the end of *The End of the Affair*. Like a bird of paradise fed on dung beetles, a spider ruined on rice wine, a wormhole inside a worm, a porcupine in a bubble, a scalpel in a cake—like blood in a storm cloud, like eyelids on a rainbow. Like even if this was enough, it wouldn't be enough. Like this looks like what it is. Looks like fingers in hair. Looks like pea soup. Looks like bulldozers. Smells like hospitals. Sounds like ghosts, laughing. Tastes like chicken. Looks like rain.

NOCTURNE

The notion of a premature death is dishonest. Like
there was something needed doing that because of it
won't get done. Like anyone has anything to do. Like
the fuzz on a baby's head need frame a face before
it falls out. Like we aren't the same person, and all
our last meals gratuitously over-seasoned. And it's
only when I wake up in the morning that I know I'm
nocturnal. That the receding glacier is frivolous. That
carbon dioxide will find its way out. Imagine that on
your way to the gallows, instead of stepping aside
to avoid a puddle, you dive in and break your neck.
What a thing never to have happened. And there we
were. Up to no good in each other's bodies. Up to our
necks in our severed heads.

ROUTES

From time to time: more time. No duration I felt has ever made up for its being made up. What I plan to do tomorrow is work in reverse to arrive at this exact point. So take my life to pieces and build a faster circuit. Take my life, and fill it with whatever's left. Eventually, I want the same afterwards that came before it. You know the stuff. Lucretius gave it symmetry. The proto-nihilists sunbathing by the shore: they were sweating it. So we learn without learning. So we learn not all roads lead to Rome: some, we learn, run in less than perfect circles round Milan.

SOLIDS

If we see it coming it won't happen. We will all be butchered in this fog. Quiet! Listen! Can anyone hear the soughing of a lung? Is it disembodied like the bodies we were in? Excuse my hands: I'm going to feel my way around. Is that you, already hanging from a tree? What was it I had to do? I give up. I give up the way I know how (but without the knowhow), the way religions are born.

BEYONDS WITH THIS HOUR

Where am I going, when my weariness is everywhere? said no astronaut ever. And so what if I gamified boredom; like Ionesco's hermit, I got to do it sitting down. Conveniently, watching my desires perish one by one was the last desire I had. Mine is not a culture of despair: a culture of despair inoculates— inoculates against despair, against the possibility of any one of us despairing. Remember, when the gods are angry nothing changes. Is it just me, or is everyone else just talking to themselves? Apparently, the post-apocalypse has nothing to do with the sudden inconceivability of mail. But coincidentally this isn't strictly true. Ennui is not what it used to be. I reminisce: such a very quiet voice for such a many-headed beast. How does a letter or a word destroy the world? And who gets to decide which one? In the beginning was an articulate aphasia, and what never got said is where I'm going.

RHYMING PANG

I have my suicidal ideation pipetted onto two glass slides. I make a wire frame and wear them over my eyes, so that all my afterlives become my current lives—I use them up concurrently. Every day the same axioms, the same witchcraft of the same body. I leak moonlight from lunchtime and know that nobody is coming. I blame my prenatal exposure to naivety; I blame its cruel resilience and its fragility. I have 50 ice ages under my belt. I have a theory I'm working on starving out my host—of me. But more than anything, and at least, I know it's the island that's unstable, not the sea.

AN EXILE

If I can choose to find a rat fetus in the bloodstream of a horse, then what use to me is this room cleaned of spiders without a door? You spew societal collapse, I drink it to the greater good. I'll spoof your spoofing until we're all one person, and too full of ourselves to get into heaven. Come on, don't ask me to believe in anything; it's too late, much too late. I'm tired: I've been up for years. And I care, I do, but it's just so many people waiting to find out where their cancer will arrive. You catch it early, you catch it late; I caught your slipperiness as a boy, and I haven't dropped it yet.

EMPORIUM

Santa Claus doesn't care if you die in a burqa or a bikini. It's all the same to him. He's pleased to see you whatevertheexcuse:yourearthquakeunpreparedness, your wrong planet wrong thermonuclear war. His catastrophometer is calibrated such that everybody's death is the death of a solipsist. Contrary to the fable, there's no discrimination behind the beard: he's assembled mourners for a horse-molester, a parasite, a poisoner; he's mapped the wind to Ho-Ho-Ho just the right amount of teargas every time. The fatness of his belly is high art. His face has grazed the tundra so that yours doesn't have to. He is his own perennial return, and the promise of this present to everybody else. He is the brain injury of a life that's never going away. He is this ecstasy and this doom. He is the emperor of plastic.

MEMORANDUM

Insomnia is a seminary school for pessimists. When it comes to death I'm not for sale. My brain's reward pathways know I'm uncomfortable with praise. If you want to get me off, I'm going to need a pornography that's less anatomical more astronomical. I'm fertile with whatever's sterile. My insensitivity is touch-sensitive. My incentives are undernourished. This virtual reality headset is a faster horse.

HALF-LIFE

Those lives spent on fentanyl, I'm not sure I see the waste. I hear only the testimonies of people. In acts I and 2 of *The Seagull*, it is Konstantin who is delusional. By the end of act 4, he's the only one who isn't. Whatever it is we're talking about, let's not kid ourselves we're getting better at it. I get away, I reconnoitre a nuclear reactor; its decay is the warmth I need. There is state-sanctioned murder in the Philippines. Anyone using illegal drugs can be killed legally. Who knew it would come to something? Who knew the price of escape was freedom?

MY FAVOURITE NOSEBLEED

The landscape isn't there. I'm uneasy with the ring of truth this has and my being outside of it. I stand on the empty cigarette packets of the anxious, and the view hasn't changed. Beyond what I can think are the gas fields of some other state, and its pipelines blocked with human excrement. As it stands, I refuse to die for this being alive, for the price on my head in a currency I don't understand. Worth noting: all the meltwater of all the glaciers won't quench the thirst of our latest abstractions. Come polish my tusks! Come chew my abortion pills! The far enemy is due west of Proxima Centauri and facing the other way.

PROSTHETICS

The prostheses are learning our humanities. The legs are going gammy, and someone has spotted gangrene in a hand. The arteries of the hearts are hardening. The breast implants are turning cancerous. The retinas one by one are going blind. My son tells me he cannot imagine the nothing of what it means to die, but that he cannot imagine anything else there either. All his limbs and organs are prosthetic in all but name. And nothing I say, but the pockets of blue light that put him back to sleep.

STAIRWELLS

What I have, I wonder, could I sweat it out in a stairwell in Manila? We are all of us indigenous refugees. We come here with nothing, we leave with a headache. We sleep on concrete floors. The woman on the floor below is in bits, but her children are together. I romanticize the remotest places as a way of staying artificial. I blame my metabolic disorder: I'm shitting out bits of animals I never ate. A man in the stairwell says I have the complexion of a cinder block. I take it as a compliment: it's the look I'm going for, or the inverse of that. Turns out the sun was never where he found it. And it was never the sun. Turns out a stairwell can be anywhere; and as long as you spell it correctly, nobody can tell.

THIS COMPARATIVE SAMENESS

I'm going to think myself into a state of harmony. Remember how certitude came to us in the form of contradictions? Remember that time when the zombie didn't attack, when it was just confused, like it had forgotten what it was? Remember how it looked melancholic for a moment, as if recalling its former life? Imagine the comparison it made. Imagine inhabiting that earlier, contrasted state—without ever losing the disparity. The comic says *I'm dying here*, and everybody laughs.

DIAGNOSTICS

I've consumed my own body weight in weight-loss tablets. I tell myself a lifelong flirtation doesn't constitute marriage, that I can let this shit go. I've seen how they send them home once the final diagnosis has been made. I know what an end-of-life package looks like. A man disowns what's left for the sake of an armchair. His bowel sits inside the cancer it made. The cannibal in the mirror is off his food. Tell them I come from a long line of pre-teen suicides. Tell them to bury me in a salt mine, and come get me when I'm cured.

EMPTY INTERIORS

We all have the same life-threatening condition, but some of us are stealing organs. Some of us think we need those organs more than someone else. Some of us can hear ourselves think, and have more organs than we know what to do with. If only my gut bacteria would tell me what it wants. If only removing the infrastructure associated with thought would leave something else. I already miss the eyes I have, and there are only a small handful of organs I could juggle without dropping. The moon was falciform when I compared it to my inability to take celestial bodies at face value. The idea, I guess, is to make what's empty appear full: like atoms, like malnourished bellies, like ambiguity.

COLLAPSE NOISE

I dreamt I was at a dream conference, where I'd fallen asleep and was dreaming I was somewhere else, dreaming I was at a dream conference. I'm trying to explain the circularity of a circle before it's too late. I'm trying before the curvature of the earth isn't curved anymore. Most humans are designed to mimic other humans, however alien that might seem. The mantra says how the vanished can still be heard— and seen. Say something enough times and you will start to believe in the relative importance of saying over what is said. Can anybody else hear the sound of the poets resuscitating their prose? The noise is so distinctive that it can't be likened to anything else— except perhaps the collapse noise of leopards killed in automobile accidents, and the alarming frequency of that.

LOGISTICS

By the time we were ready to leave we'd already considered what would happen if we ever arrived. But then not all artificial skins are artificial. They call it the nocebo effect. We take painkillers. We take immunosuppressants. We even try conventional breeding. There are more intangible details than our near-permanent concussion can explain. It was difficult to recognize ourselves at first; but we took pictures with our phones, and the algorithm confirmed that we were there. We do not dream of ending up someplace. We dream about the dream we might have, one afternoon, while only pretending to be asleep.

A VISIT TO HERE

Getting lost in the cracks didn't seem important: a small particulate matter. We found, though, we healed faster when they dehumanized us slower. And those materials that mimicked non-materials carried on hiding us, even after they'd cut them into the thinnest slices. We were, it seems, virtually indistinguishable from our virtual disappearance. Where we ended up escaping to was a place they called an evolutionary dead end. It is why there are fewer sightings in the future. It is what happens. When the former synergism of veracity and insight finally collapse into the same thing, what happens is that we don't have to.

CONCERNING THIS

I didn't see that coming is how I remember the future.
It used to come in sections. I'd be cramped until the
next; so now, to mitigate the claustrophobia, I get
smaller year on year. Biopsy after biopsy and the
results never come back. Muscle memory is how I
got this old. To understand what is happening, for
a split-second I'm not everything I could be. This
almost universal covenant with reality only means
there's less to go around. The surface is deeper than
you think: it's surface all the way down. The view of
the horizon is unspoiled. I look away to see there's
nothing there.

CONTINGENT ON

The way the accident kills is clever: it gets away with it every time. Conviction as a prelude to exoneration: the last time I laughed this hard I broke my leg. It's no coincidence that I laugh the same way hyenas eat impalas: bones and all. It's no coincidence that the anthropic principle appeals to just the right kind of humans—in more than thirty variations. I practice pre-emptive surprise as a way of hearing my own voice. But try circumventing your confirmation bias, and it'll rip your throat out. The sequel to the accident is not another accident.

THE OTHERNESS OF OTHERNESS

Nothingness is contaminated by all its different renderings. For instance, what happens to the number of road deaths the minute we stop counting? What happens to what doesn't have words when it can't be outsourced to God? And to his silence, no less. I eat insects by mistake but never megafauna. I outnumber myself by a factor of somewhere between zero and minus-one. If it doesn't add up it's because I can't count. And yet, all this: it's just so much pangolin quaffed in the dark. To get me through, no more, can you tell me something positive, apophatically speaking? Too much to ask, with nothing to say, I know, but still. Someday something will be what it seems. I'm advised not to, but I'm holding my breath.

NOT THE ONE YOU GIVE

No one here knows the names of the flowers in the hospital grounds. My mouth waters on the words, and nothing grows. Inside, designer babies are coming out sideways. I hear they're too worn out from the all the effort to cry. The ward I'm waiting in is the quiet of everyone struggling to breathe. There are 10,000 genetic variants and what we can't know isn't one of them. Disaffected doctors play peekaboo behind disinfected hands. I'm here for a brain transplant. I'm here for my convalescence as someone else. I ask myself, Is this early onset rigor mortis? I ask myself, Where have you become?

TEMPORAL INDIGESTION

The trouble with not being born is a problem I can live with. I've said it again and I've said it before: presentism is the new presentism. My time-travelling always ends the same way: my parents dead at the hands of a paradox. I'm here in the future and the past is so cancer it's not even unreal. The future's on a loop. The future's so yesterday. We're all dying to say something before someone else notices.

COMMUNITY

It's not what I envisaged, but my near-death experience seems to be getting further away. The fox in my garden is chewing up the lawn, and for a moment he is everything I want him to be. The nausea of my neighbours' happiness is being vomited into plastic bags. We have the mutual self-awareness of our silence. None of us will ever have anything more profound to say than this. Our banal perfection, cum perfect banality, was allowed to exist and nothing else came close.

VIRAL

There's something almost homely about a giant virus in Siberia that's waited till now to wake up. I think of it like the Capgras syndrome I've been trying to cultivate—as if I wouldn't love the imposters just as much. You see, it's all nerve agents out there, and my gas mask is fogging up. I was counting the dead bodies amassed in the Grand Canyon, and that had something to do with it. They were everyone that had ever lived. The sight of billions of dead anything is vernacular for the superficiality of giving anyone what they want. Poetry is impossible or it isn't. Its possibility is a joke. It would be like actually laughing out loud. Like a vacuum with nothing in it.

OUTSIDE AESTHETICS

The percussion of monsoon rains on black tarpaulins. A bullet hole in the back of him in the rice paddy. The main problem with believers is that they don't really believe. The glow of smartphones at the edge of a forest. Queues of the immiserated growing. The killer on my screen has a necklace of teeth. The soldiers took turns, she said. That there remains a need for ambiguity is not restricted to theoretical concerns within aesthetics. The soldiers took turns, she said, and we listened like we knew.

WHAT WE GET TO SEE

As their if-then signatures become ever more uniform, they recognize themselves in increasingly diverse ways. Their acoustic facility becomes attuned to feedback at the expense of most other things. They self-harm, when situations demand, only according to prescribed collateral patterns. The weather on the outskirts of their homes is invariably humid: they regulate their body temperature so they won't have to faint. If they ask to see their records, only heavily redacted versions will be available. The surprise will come when we don't see more of this.

INAPPROPRIATE COSTUME

When the machines try to speak for us, won't they say too much? If they come to get us, will they even comprehend the space we're in? Rilke warns of the machine, abhors its clatter and its impudence. But is the machine any more emphatic than the tree? Or the bear climbing up it, with me at the top? Are these electrodes implanted in my brain any more offensive than the autoimmune condition of my soul? And aren't the living also exhausted by purpose (in both senses of the phrase), and unspeakable, and unspeakably ugly? I stumble over the names of brain diseases, and I can't get up.

THE END OF LUNCH, ALMOST

The word *almost* will become synonymous with *never*, and nothing will ever be very important again. The way the word *almost* sucks out all the air of whatever comes after it gets me every time. In its wake I am almost redeemed. I am almost the very thing that thought itself into existence. Also, almost for no reason, there will be exactly too many terms meaning death, that when analysed turn out not to mean death at all, but some vaguely inadequate memory of it—too many misdirections to it. They will circumnavigate it in inventive ways. My own death will dangle like the modifiers I've come to use. Standing on my head, the ivy mistakes me for a tree. And I almost made it, I mean it: I almost got to say whatever it is I've said.

THE EXPERIMENT

We permuted a cephalopod to make it think like a human. And we waited and we watched and nothing happened. It behaved in all the ways we'd come to expect from observing countless cephalopods over countless years. It moved and ate and bred the same as all the others. It changed colour to match the environment, and whether or not it was colour blind it didn't say. When in a final, exasperated effort to witness some deviation, we turned ourselves inside out, the cephalopod turned the very colour for which we had no name.

DAISY

My grandmother starved herself to death. Apparently, eating the smoke of 60 cigarettes a day does not meet the nutritional requirements needed to do anything else. The outlook was more moments aggregating into longer moments and all the consumption that involved. Like Kafka's fasting artist, who never found a food he liked, she made a talent of revulsion and played it out. But there's no art in subjugation to oneself, in succumbing to who you are. There's honesty, there's truth, there's bravery, perhaps; but nothing worth dying for, when you can make it up. After all, I've eaten all my life and look at me: a reed of smoke still imagining it might die.

SKINNED ALIVE

The thin air of high altitudes and all this tonnage of meat. The paranoia of a city in the pelt of a leopard. I remember seeing the marble statue of Saint Bartholomew flayed in the Duomo di Milano. I remember my wife being denied entry, because her shoulders were on display. And now the head and skin of a lion in a box. We get the conservationists we deserve. We get the apostles someone else deserved. We get to be offended by the body parts of our choice. In sum, I'll take extinctions over your quanta of expedient suffering any day. Tell me, when you live forever, will you dissect my corpse with such a loving eye? Will I weigh enough to constitute a miracle? Will I be worth my weight in souls? Evening comes, a tiger drinks from a bowl of tiger bone wine, and disappears.

CODA

How is it your horrors are not mine? And how is it that they are? Trying to exchange suffering for words is like marking your own homework, and still getting it wrong. It's not true that genetically engineered mice will improve our nightmares. They can't even sing in a straight line. Not that your expectations were high, but this illegal trade in miserablist anecdotes isn't as lucrative as you might think. As soon as I'm destitute enough I plan on being happy with all the things I don't have. Right now I have a terabyte of examples that show how examples are misleading. Right now this something on the edge of my experience is ten times the size of itself. It's a kind of uncomfortably dimensioned kind of thing. My incompleteness is about the size of its confusion. Encompassing this uncertainty, as a strain of precision, I repeat myself until the only meaning left is modulation. I get up from my chair. I go in no directions at once.

ABOUT THE AUTHOR

Gary J. Shipley is the author of numerous books, including *Stratagem of the Corpse: Dying With Baudrillard* (Anthem), *30 Fake Beheadings* (Spork), and *Warewolff!* (Hexus). He has been published in many literary magazines, anthologies and academic journals, and is the founding and managing editor of Schism Press. More information can be found at Thek Prosthetics.

ELEVEN 11:11 ELEVEN PRESS

11:11 Press is an American independent literary publisher based in Minneapolis, MN. Founded in 2018, 11:11 publishes innovative literature of all forms and varieties. We believe in the freedom of artistic expression, the realization of creative potential, and the transcendental power of stories.

www.ingramcontent.com/pod-product-compliance
Lightning Source LLC
LaVergne TN
LVHW041229080426

835508LV00011B/1126